The Ohio State University Press/*The Journal* Award in Poetry

The River Won't Hold You

Karin Gottshall

The Ohio State University Press
Columbus

Library of Congress Cataloging-in-Publication Data
Gottshall, Karin, author.
 The river won't hold you / Karin Gottshall.
    pages cm
"Ohio State University Press/The journal award in poetry."
 ISBN 978-0-8142-5189-8 (pbk. : alk. paper) — ISBN 978-0-8142-9374-4 (cd-rom)
 I. Title.
 PS3607.O88R58 2014
 811'.6—dc23
                         2014020124

Cover design by Mia Risberg
Text design by Juliet Williams
Type set in Janson
Printed by Thomson-Shore, Inc.

9   8   7   6   5   4   3   2   1

For my grandmothers:

Norma Groves Andrew
Mary Evans Gottshall

Contents

II.

III.

Acknowledgments

Grateful acknowledgment is made to the editors of the following journals and websites where these poems first appeared:

Augury Books Blog: Love Poem with Ebb Tide
Blackbird: Once
The Collagist: Cathedral Cities
Crazyhorse: Forecast; Lesson
Devil's Lake: Mending
Failbetter: The Wasted Years
FIELD: Raven
The Gettysburg Review: The Consolation of Philosophy; Pretty Stories
The Greensboro Review: Eve; The Snow House
Harvard Review: Blink Once
The Journal: Departure; Yellow House Poem
Juked: Soap
Memorious: Earthquake; Faith
Michigan Quarterly Review: To Celia: 2
Mid-American Review: Circus; Listening to the Dead
New Ohio Review: More Lies
New South: Satellite; The weather is a better companion and by that I don't just mean
La Petite Zine: Ghost Story
The Same: Love Poem with Darkened Lamps
Sentence: A Journal of Prose Poetics: Rain
The Southern Review: To Celia: 1; To Celia: 3
Spoon River Poetry Review: The Sliver
Tar River Poetry Review: The River Child
The Virginia Quarterly Review: Virginity
West Branch: Household Gods; Operative

The following poems were included in the chapbook *Swan* (Argos Books, 2014):

> Forecast; The Tiger; Faith; Vespers; Parochial; Circus; Soap; Lesson; Virginity; Pretty Stories; Earthquake; Blink Once; To Celia: 1; To Celia: 2; To Celia: 3; To Celia: 4; Eve; Once; The Sliver; After all, the river; Conception.

The author also wishes to acknowledge the help and support of several friends, family members, and colleagues: Paige Ackerson-Kiely, Penelope Cray, Marybeth Gottshall, Tim Gottshall, Kerrin McCadden, Cindy Hunter Morgan, Alison Prine, Terry Simpkins, The Department of English and American Literatures at Middlebury College, and the Creative Writing Program at Interlochen Center for the Arts.

"Father—" is dedicated to Claire Sibley, whose use of the word "disconsolate" in a poem provided inspiration.

Thanks to Wyn Cooper for his friendship and editorial help.

Thanks to Kathy Fagan for selecting this manuscript and to everyone at OSU Press for their patience and guidance in the process of turning it into a book.

Thanks and love to Jeff Stauch.

Forecast

I remember thinking, before the snow started,
I wish it would start. The sky darkened

shadow on shadow. The cats, as usual,
slept through the morning. Then snow so heavy that even

my father, who was a kind of Noah—all resolve and solitude,
cabinetry and salt—couldn't have steadied me. I remember—

and this was back when the sham fortune-teller sat
turning over cards, saying *you will be lonely*—

thinking it could be worse. Thinking loneliness
is nothing more than a cotton slip

and uncombed hair. A path you dig in the snow
once the snow has stopped. Thinking *then let it begin.*

I.

Lesson

At some location between the rod
and the hook, which shot straight
on its filament through the locust-sung
summer air (sun-blistered
and clover-hung), at the flick
of her cousin's right wrist, until it reached
the soft crease of her inner elbow where
it snagged and he laughed (she cried out)—
that tender purchase of dart in flesh
allowing him to reel her bleating back
along a taut line of animal pain
she couldn't unfasten from—at some
point along that axis humming casual
violence (and his boy heat and her blood
just beginning to bubble under the barb),
a false idea she had about this world
and her position in it was corrected.

The Tiger

Childhood was years of swallowing schoolroom clocks
like big aspirin tablets. Matching up blue socks hot

from the dryer. I was sometimes worried God
could see me when I stepped into the tub,

sometimes worried he couldn't.
I learned the moon is a monastic,

exiled from the commerce of the earth. Our shirts
were made of softest starjuice. In the hundred

years I was nine I solved ten thousand math problems
but no one asked me what I loved, so I just

unbuckled my shoes each night, alone with it.
Places in the tall grass where the deer have lain.

A bird flying up when you didn't know it was there.
I sat on the bench outside the stained glass

of the First Universalist, pretending I was inside. Tried
to pray for less shyness: what the old people called

making strange. Wide-open, staring eyes of the tiger
I drew and had to destroy because it wouldn't sleep.

Faith

Playing alone, I would duchess the clothesline:
empty sleeves in the wind's gentle harness.

An only child weighing one form of solitude
against another. Walking between buildings

there was sometimes a feeling of floating up—
piano music from an open window. Given milk

with a little coffee mixed in, given a rosary
by mistake; I felt closer to God in Canada,

maybe because of the lake. My grandmother
took me to Zeller's and bought me a nightgown

with lace. Everyone is so tired. I have never
understood it. Canoeing to the island I lost

a tooth. *You're a big kid now*, the cousins
scolded, and snag went my tongue on the space.

Vespers

How easy to blame all our troubles on the cold snap.
Confused about the nature of things I thought
my shadow was some kind of undergarment,

always slipping out, and therefore I confounded
it with the ritual of church-going. The whole construct
anchored by the smell of camphor. Pantyhose

hanging from the shower curtain reminded me
of rain, of that gauzy comet-tail, the legs of deer
stealthy in the conifers. Would I ever have grand-

daughters: a question I sometimes asked the humidifier.
That was the winter of my sickliness—how easy
to blame it all on weather. I would have preferred prayer,

but like most of my letters I could only begin
with apologies. My shadow on the ceiling, the little
tramp, so transparent. I would have preferred

less screaming in my fever-dreams. Each time
I played church I turned the wooden knob
on the jack-in-the-box, my makeshift pipe organ, and God

was in the room. Gratitude in my lungs. It is not a service
I can replicate or deem holy with any real certainty.

Parochial

My ancestors built their whalebone corsets
at home, but I haven't worn a slip since 1976.
The translucence of certain kinds of moth
wings, of stained glass, dried fluids. Swaying
to the radio, eyes closed, praying
before bed. The jar I dropped pennies into, the toast,
the unopened box of sparkplugs rusting
in the basement. Was I a person who would
one day reach forty: a question I sometimes asked
the oven. Putting on my underwear every morning
(whales harpooned for the bones against the bones
of my great-grandmother, her own soft and lonely mother).
A catechism of thistles, skipping to school
followed by black and white cats like Sister
Marys and Josephines. At home my mother built
her paintings while the Stones brayed, left her bras
on the bedside table. They were the color
of swans, the color, I guessed, of God's
thoughts. Milk and cinnamon and supplications
—the standard slip I slept in and outgrew.

Circus

I was drawn as though to blood-rites: stripes
rising up over heat ripples, smell of hay,
and inside all those delicate wires for the body
to harness and balance on. In my seat, I picked a blister
on my palm until it popped, a spent purse.

My eyes stung from gunpowder, horse piss.
So this is the state of childhood, I thought,
as my father tied a balloon string around my wrist. Sticky
sugar on my jeans. Smell of sweat and the ringmaster
with a full day's beard. I was simply too old and too sad,

first cramps circling in me like rusty wheels, but I'll say
this: I couldn't look away from those wire-walkers—poised
over emptiness with bored faces—nor fire-eaters,
nor the woman who contorted on a silk skein:
slipping so fluidly through her own knots.

Soap

It is full bitter winter when I begin
to bleed. Too ashamed to tell. Aligning myself
with the crows I take the back way home.
Pages of book reports blown down the hill.
What constitutes anger is passion plus a disappointment
of hopes. Bad math. The body plus the smell
of burning. The Pine-Sol ghost of the school hall
and early mornings I can't wake up. The fluorescent
bulb was invented for us, and the closed window.
Moths hatching from the flour. I have the most tender
feeling and nowhere to apply it. Superstitious, I walk
only where the path is most difficult, stack my pennies
by year, nurse a private longing for fancy soaps.
Monthly this extra thing I can't use, and meanwhile
so much else I can't have. Candles lit
on the windowsills when my mother can't pay
the electric bill. We make the best of it, all that soft light.

Virginity

The weather was all that changed
after I lost it. I sat curled in the blue
armchair at the free library, reading *Orlando*.
Outside the trees lived and moved

amid the wind's coils and autumn slipped,
day by day, toward winter. After school
I watched the fragile projection
of the film club's silents: Mary Pickford's slim

waist, her delicate face enclosed in a locket.
Inexpert piano and the other kids drifting off
over their homework. For months
I wore the same black tights on Tuesdays,

a snag above the left knee, and sometimes
it seemed my heart spread and stung
like a sea-creature, filling me with salt.
The sensual life whose arrival I'd awaited,

whose tenure I'd anticipated with words
like *grace*, was the tired old cat purring
against my chest, oatmeal and rough wool
in the morning, cool rain to my skin.

Pretty Stories

Ophelia, in her flip-flops, writes her paramour's name
against the dusk with the spitting tip of a sparkler wand.

Meanwhile, the cat leaves a narrow tongue-print
on the butter Mother forgot to put away after lunch,

and two blocks down the children pursue
an ice cream truck's canned *Yankee Doodle Dandy.*

They say the owl was a baker's daughter;
here's rue for you and a-down, a-down-a.

True: we were all fooled by Viola the time she dressed
as a pirate and made out with Olivia under the bleachers.

In candlelight Hermia and Helena get out their makeup
kits to blacken their eyelids and shine their lips.

The pet hamsters weigh almost nothing; in the morning
they will turn into soap bubbles and rise over the roofs.

Prospero tells Miranda the same story every night:
water filled the sailors' mouths with brine

and if you think it's hot here, you should visit
the belly of the beast. Roses, my love. The end.

Earthquake

When I tell you my childhood was wasted
at sea, you should bear in mind
I may be an unreliable narrator.

When I say I spent a year
in military school, disguised as a boy,
be skeptical—though in fact I did.

Each morning we polished our boots
to an oily sheen and ran through the spruce
woods with empty guns. When I tell you

I love white wine, it's the plain truth.
As is the fact that my mother
was a painter and my father a cellist—

or a physicist. I get the two confused.
I get confused about the relative
weight of my loneliness: it seems so heavy,

but where is it? Did you know I survived
shipwreck? That I was marooned
and lived a long time on the island? Surely

that explains this hook-shaped scar,
my love of salt. I ask for no help
with these burdens. The earthquake rocked,

rocked the building's foundation
and the bedposts swayed
like masts. We set off from port. All my lies

are like that: they travel
so far over the horizon, then finally
come back: my sea-weary, long lost kin.

Blink Once

At fifteen I was what's called bookish—
I had a recurring dream of an owl
lecturing on the surrealists,

and I always woke from it happy.
I spent that entire summer running
the projector in the library basement—

silent movies for the kids on vacation,
cold coffee and fritters on a table
for the grownups. The films were fragile

and old and everyone laughed
when Buster Keaton fell in love. I had
the whole day to think and my thoughts

all felt sculpted, I worked that hard
on each one—chiseled and rasped.
I spent evenings reading in my room,

listening to thunder. Sometimes a firefly
would stray through the broken screen
and I'd wake in the night to its beacon,

its clumsy flight. I'd say oh, Buster Keaton,
I'm still too young and our love
is forbidden. Your body's a lamp

and I'm a boat far out at sea.
Can you wait for me, my moonbeam, my
daffodil? Blink once if you will.

To Celia

1

We're flat on our backs, reading *The Tempest*.
Autumn light fills your room, woodsmoke smell drifts
in through the open window. Your dog shifts
and sighs. We pity Caliban. The test
is tomorrow. We're both Miranda, seques-
tered in stifling adolescence. You sift
through your closet, its fragile loot of thrift-
store finds and antiques. To study we'll dress
in airy scarves and cowboy boots, pretend
we're Ariel, recite the lines, such stuff
as dreams are made on. Behold the faux-pearled
maidens, exiled to the bustling earth's end,
eating peanut butter and marshmallow fluff.
You laugh, kiss my sunburnt hand. Brave new world.

To Celia

2

When rain rattled the walnut tree we lit
candles and set up the Ouija board
to contact your cousin Beth. She'd transmit
lines of pop songs, gossip, sow quick discord
between realms. A depressive spirit, she
wasn't one to answer the big questions:
when queried on the afterlife she'd plead
the fifth, ask about the current fashions.

Heaven seemed immeasurably distant
and not all that interesting. Mystery
was conversation, sex, the strange present
tense: how particular, how unlikely.
We put away the heart planchette. We said
it seemed weirder to be alive than dead.

To Celia

3

You brought a pomegranate from New York.
I'd missed you. Soft December snowflakes more
wandered than fell. We went outside at dark
to eat it, digging into the flesh core
with our nails, spilling red juice on the snow.
It made me think of biting into bees—
that sting of sweetness in the cold, the slow
numbing of my tongue. *You vampire*, I teased—
your mouth was crimson with it. It dripped down
our arms, itching under wool sweater sleeves.
So had Persephone, tempted, eaten fruit grown
in the lonely underworld of Hades
and lifted winter's burden, a little:
her hunger less keen, her heart less brittle.

To Celia

4

We're walking your dog on the wooded trail
behind the free library—it's green spring,

the frogs are singing and the lacy, frail
shoots of the first ferns are uncoiling.

There's a place back here, among roots of oak
and bracken, like a little secret den

we call the witchy bower, where we smoke
and sing too loud and make our confessions.

You lift your skirt to show me the marbled bruise
some boy left. *Come live with me and be my love,*

you say, *and we will all the pleasures prove.*
Red squirrels quarrel in the branches above.

We're holding hands and a moth, spring azure,
settles jewel-like against your long black hair.

Eve

All I had was the doe's rib bone—
found by the lake, beside the shards
of vertebrae seeding themselves in the mud—

but I talked to her like she was whole,
could hear. I was seventeen. It was a way I had
of praying, I think. Because I'd read

the story of Eve and knew I would make
the same choice, already knew how it felt
to choose wrongly just to see how far regret

would take me. It was light as a breath.
I kept it on the windowsill with candles
and snail shells. I'm sure there's a better religion

for my troubles but it's what I had,
and her rib was fragile as a child's. Her afterlife
was everywhere—there was nothing

that didn't contain it—I told her that
again and again while darkness whiskered
at the house and the curtains filled with wind.

And when I finally thought I understood
I dropped it in the lake: into the mineral
solution that accepts whatever is offered.

Once

I won't start with once
upon a time. Because that's the whole

story isn't it, lovely as she was
with her hair like honey? She bled

alone on the bed when he'd left
and the queen set her to work threading

needles in the dark. She saw
what she shouldn't have: beauty

in the place of a serpent, and that's when
she learned regret. The three drops

of tallow on his skin or the moment
the weather changed and she wished

for wings. Then a dress of rags
and the rough stones of the brook.

The whiskered fish and the trees
casting their dark shadows. I won't

start with once—the girl
on the bed, bleeding—the task of dowsing,

the long search for the mouth
of the underworld and the lover

with his scent of apple flesh and musk.
The time it takes to turn

away—one breath—and her body
clenched around its knot of hunger.

The Sliver

I tease it out with tweezers—
narrow dagger of glass, tipped
with the thin rusty veneer

of my blood. The wound bubbles:
a small red mouth at my heel.
Just when I start to feel

like a rational human being
something like this has to happen—
a sharp insertion sending shivers

all through me—but the body
is a messy instrument
with its groping senses

and aversions. They say the girl
locked in a chamber with only
a thin splinter of an opening

was entered and impregnated
by a blade of light. Children
whisper that glass in the bloodstream

pierces the heart. For the first time,
now, I notice it's spring: the needles
soften on the evergreens

and in the trees the crimson
wedges of the cardinals call
their song's sharp, clear incisions.

After all, the river

won't hold you, pushes you firmly
to the bank. Flowers dot the grass like loose
change. You're wearing the dress
with rickrack, yellow oxeyes, like one your sister had
as a child.

    Once you frightened yourself, pulling
    too much sweetness from the body
    of your violin with your bow.

    You touched yourself when
    there was no one else to do it; even when
    there was.

When no arms can soothe you
there are weeds: fluids
gather at dark openings. A body
in the weeds: if this is death it was easy
in coming, and after all
it's only a little less.

Conception

Girl curled around your book,
Go outside to the tamaracks.

Untie your shoes.

Remember the story: on the night you were conceived
Your mother dreamt of obedience;
Your milk teeth all buried beneath that tree.

In the churchyards brides and birds preen near white cake tasting like wax—
He will undress you.

Or you will row a frail boat
To a harbor near ruined temples, where honey is gathered.

The sting on your heel is soothed
By salve of the flower the bee sucked.

Loosen your hair.

It doesn't matter which you begin with—
Either way, your words are sealed with burnt sugar.

In the end you will have to forgive yourself.

II.

More Lies

Sometimes I say I'm going to meet my sister at the café—
even though I have no sister—just because it's such
a beautiful thing to say. I've always thought so, ever since

I read a novel in which two sisters were constantly meeting
in cafés. Today, for example, I walked alone
on the wet sidewalk, wearing my rain boots, expecting

someone might ask where I was headed. I bought
a steno pad and a watch battery, the store windows
fogged up. Rain in April is a kind of promise, and it costs

nothing. I carried a bag of books to the café and ordered
tea. I like a place that's lit by lamps. I like a place
where you can hear people talk about small things,

like the difference between azure and cerulean,
and the price of tulips. It's going down. I watched
someone who could be my sister walk in, shaking the rain

from her hair. I thought, even now florists are filling
their coolers with tulips, five dollars a bundle. All over
the city there are sisters. Any one of them could be mine.

The Wasted Years

The wasted years were filled with movies,
dreams about Venice, bread and raspberry jam.
A hundred books that drifted by
like laundry blown loose from the line,
their pages unmarked and remembered
only vaguely. I fell asleep reading. I listened
to Verdi and whole afternoons were gone.
I worked: boxing chocolate, sweeping floors,
asking would you like whipped cream on that?
There were dogs and cats: I looked
into their faces. I thought if I'd been a painter
I would have purpose now: I would paint
saints, I would paint insects, I would paint
the coffee shop filled with ghosts in the morning.
I went to art supply stores and smelled
the charcoal, bought myself thick blank books
that were never filled. My shoes wore out
and I found another pair just the same. My recipe
for peace was a baked pear and my remedy
for sorrow was a smoke. My friends called
at regular intervals and we spoke about the past
as though it were a puzzle we had yet to solve.
I lay in the sun and didn't care what happened.
Birdsong poured like sticky liquid from the trees
and stuck one moment to the next, and I felt
my life adhere and slide like syrup as I fell asleep
under the thousand shades of green.

Luxury

A letter arrived from Wales and I
never opened it. That was my one
luxury, before the cherry blossoms opened

in the park. It was the spring I had
a broken heart and a neighbor who played
Greensleeves every night on her violin.

I dyed my hair blue, then bluer. I think
of Wales as a country of sailors and shepherds.
My ancestors came from there, long ago, and once

I visited: a castle on the edge of the Irish Sea.
Very delicate cups of tea. The sheep
were so shy on the hillsides: I think

I am generalizing. I don't even know
for sure that it was a letter. I thought of the bells
and the pints of beer. The sailors.

The envelope was thin and white as a petal,
a blossom from a distant tree. My one luxury:
it was enough it was addressed to me.

Sister—

Purple throats of the spring ephemerals
open beside the concrete stoop. After four days
of damp, raw cold, this morning is hazy
with heat. Dozing, I dream of the day we swam
between cool granite walls, small fingers sliding
over slick stones of the quarry. The dead speak

in colors: a synesthesia whose grammar
of iris and aster I stumble over. And so
must imagine you tongueless, entombed—
lamprey coiled beneath our lazy kicking
feet. Speckled mouths full of rain.

Cathedral Cities

I wanted to make a dress
from the hotel curtains. I wanted
to keep a diary. All those delicate bridges
and the cathedrals like the insides of flowers.
I slept alone in a man's pajama top.
The map didn't mind being held
upside-down: it was shaped like a fish. Once
I passed two women talking. Iris
is fourteen today, the tall one said, and I
thought of Iris all night on the train. How painful
to be fourteen. In the morning I couldn't
find coffee and I did my laundry using strange coins.
In every church Mary held her white hands
open. Doors wide to the wind. I stood
by the side of a river whose name
I've forgotten, and for once
the stars were right where I'd left them.

Even Forty

I'm still just a girl, just a donkey
of sorts. I have this soft

mouth. In the morning, for
two full hours, I resemble

my mother. I am a woman
in space—a spacewalker!

My first jewel was beveled plastic.
I stand in the lamplight, wearing

a slip. It's winter and the raccoons
are hibernating. Rose hips

drum against the aluminum
shed. They were sent into space,

the satellites, and they died.
Wink, wink, there's a blue light

blinking above the clouds—
I haven't got a string of pearls.

No lovers, no magazines. I
gave them away to the saints.

Father—

By this time that year I'd already lost a sandal
in the stream. I wanted only to be as clear
as the girl on the bus who carried a satchel of music,
a small stringed instrument in its case.
Afternoons spent watching poppies smolder.
But your indifference made a creature that panics equally
in the face of anger and desire.

Deer pick their way over rubble
unearthed by the backhoe. Once I slept
over the ocean, in a pressurized cabin bound
for Rome, where poppies burned at the base
of Vesta's temple. Summer begins again, disconsolate,
scrolling through storm cells. And you
kept me penned, animal that I was.

Permission

It's the time of year for finding the dry shell of a cicada clinging to the sheet left overnight on the laundry line. The creature itself watches from the branches, green and damp beneath the wings. It's so great to be forty, to wear complicated underclothes and fantasize about rinse cycles, to go without sleep. To guiltlessly leave the laundry tensing all night against the wind, regardless of the habits of insects, regardless of rain. It's so great to have the whole sky above me, a place I could inhabit if I could ditch the mineral knot of this body. Leave it drying on someone's line—that old gospel move. After so many years I can almost hear the stones inside the earth turning. I can almost hear my own impulse lapping at its subterranean banks.

Eros and the Reader

The sad truth is, I have wanted
to live inside a novel more
than I have wanted to live inside
my own life. This has been the case

since the very first novel I read, which involved
a love affair between a girl and a pig.
That old story. Since then, a lifetime
of stirring coffee with diner spoons, thinking

this is so like something in a novel!
A lifetime of moments, too,
nothing like those in books:
eating sweet potatoes for dinner every night,

letting the cat stand on the table.
There was one summer I worked in a kitchen,
sweating through my tank top; I was reading
the Brontës and grew very thin. Another summer

I was so in love I could think of nothing
except my nails on his skin. But he didn't
want me, and I went back to reading Proust.
I studied French because it's a language

so frequently spoken in books. I bought myself
a scarf that wound twelve times around
my neck because a girl in a book I read
had one. Then I let it hang loose, dragging

at my feet, waiting for the hands
that would carefully loop it under my chin.
How many times have I practiced
running on flagstones and sealing letters?

I am forever sealing letters, slowly stirring
sugar into coffee, falling in love and buying
apples. There are not enough swans
around here, though. There are not

enough heaths or swales. I lack for trains
and painters, whiskey and Sunday mornings.
Horseshoes. Hurricane lamps. Cast-iron pots,
revolvers, and gentle deft hands winding my scarf.

Mending

It took me a hundred years
just to learn to thread a needle,
and by that time all my generation

had gone, their clothes buried with them
or passed down to abler hands.
Then I set to counting buttons—so many

jars full—the navy anchors, tiny
mother-of-pearl discs no bigger
than a first tooth. I loved

to find odd things among them: antique
pen nibs, Indian arrowheads, someone's
Purple Heart. My entire life the geese

were migrating—always coming
or going—sometimes the whole sky
was stitched together with their long vees.

Sometimes, too, a fighter jet passed over
with a sound like torn cotton. The house
would shake—or maybe that was just me,

growing older. All the while I was thirsty,
and so tired—I'd finally sewed
the bedclothes closed. I wondered

when my grandmother would return
from the garden with her smell of laundry
and lemon balm, her cool steady hands.

Why I Did It

Because dusk had a habit of falling before
I'd finished putting on my mascara. Because you can't
read by the light of an onion and I'd never seen
my name written in calligraphy. Because I was so lonely
I talked to the radiators. Because home
was a series of broken Mr. Coffees and the cotton hems
of my nightgowns had all frayed. Because once
there was a fair maiden. A fair maiden who rode
the bus to her job at the supermarket. Because of the canned
peaches. And the fire. Because I've never held a full pitcher
without my wrist shaking. Never broken a bone.
Because a loose thread came teasing its way from the sleeve
of my blouse and I couldn't stop pulling.
Because I was thusly unsleeved. Because there once
was a goose girl who was only a goose girl. Because
someone's sister turned a corner and died. Because someone
else's sister never called. Because I was unconvinced
by commercials asserting my inalienable right to loveliness:
beauty like smooth milk. Because the snow came early that year
and I lay in my bed at dawn, worrying about every
single word I'd ever said. Because I said no, said yes.
Because the sky was a vintage filmstrip reel and the concrete
smelled like driving too slowly, like the fear of death.
Because the only ticket I could afford was to a city
where no one knew me and I'd never wanted to go.
Because I was pretty sure I'd eventually go there anyway.

The Consolation of Philosophy

My philosophy walks around inked
with all the tattoos I ever decided against:
delicate vine at her nape, biceps twined

with lapis patterns and black ravens,
lucky coins scattered across her belly, the sign
of Pisces at her hip. My philosophy curses

like a sailor, too, and doesn't mind
bringing strangers home—I stumble from my room
at midnight, blinking, to find her pressed

against the kitchen counter, someone's hands
in her hair, his mouth against hers—
not that my philosophy is easy.

Some mornings she chain-smokes.
"Do as I say," she says,
"not as I do." And some mornings

she sits around in her robe reading Boethius,
laughing. She says the problem
with philosophies today is they have no flair

for the dramatic, no sense of style.
She says philosophies today don't know
their business. Meanwhile, I've been thinking up

some new tattoos. "Does it hurt?" I ask.
"Not at all," she answers, smiling, stroking
the unmarked flesh of my wrist. "Pain

is *your* prerogative"—as a black bracelet
of barbed wire seeps into her,
and a serpent spirals up her calf.

Rain

Line by line the too-perfect spider-web on the back porch comes untethered. The street is strewn with leaves and spelling tests, and I go to the strip mall and back, carrying home a bag of rice.

I have the same job as everyone: counting. Someday I'll spend this coffee can of nickels. Prosperity was when I was still growing and got hand-me-downs from the church: velvet jacket, ear-flap hat.

Goodbye God, whom I met under the awning. You'll take the cross-town bus to the burnt-out factory. One long afternoon in the rain: sometimes I turn on the radio just to hear the disc jockey's voice, just to hear him breathe.

Translation

If I were tasked with inventing a language,
I would coin a term for the feeling of being called
by a different woman's name. There's another word
I wish existed, for the realization that it doesn't
matter. I may as well be that woman, and I imagine
myself into her life: perhaps at the moment
you said her name into my damp hair she was receiving
a pedicure, secure in the knowledge of your love.
There's a lesson, here, about possession: who
could be said, at that instant, to belong to whom?
If I were inventing a language there would be a word
for the woman who is simultaneously
herself, the focus of her lover's touch, and the receiver
of his other lover's name. My double mounts
the escalator, deciding which of two scents
spritzed onto separate wrists would most captivate you.
You could say it was a kind of calculation, my letting
it go. It was not. It was just one of many definitions
I bent a little, because I could not give you up.

When We Were Surrealists

To think: all through the month of October
we whispered into each others' skins. Our kisses

were like motor oil and every goose became
a monogrammed napkin en route from Montreal.

Your hands moved between my legs, the cool
breeze from the refrigerator breathed at my neck.

In November all the pastry shops went out of business
and the newspapers printed nothing but instructions

for turning their own pages into hats. December
came and you were gone—no one to cup my elbows,

no one to buy aspirin for. I sat crying
in the laundromat, reading your postcard.

It said you'd run away with the electricians' guild,
said you could never love a girl with a boomerang

tattoo. Egoist! The Pope rode by in the snow
on his bicycle, tossing peppermints and arcade tokens.

The Temple of Vesta

It must be very fine, what you're looking for,
and who am I to question the impulse
for what's beautiful and rare?
But I'm impatient with the waste—didn't I
give you honeycombs, handjobs, my body
heavy with its dreams in the morning?
I hate the profligacy that says *this and this
I'll take, every good thing you offer, but in the end
it's not enough to hold me*. As for me, I understand
desire: I've seen the women coming from the museums,
rich in shoes and self-worth, having varnished
their eyes with Vermeer. I can't say I blame you
for coveting mystery more than the big open bell
ringing its longing direct in your face. But it's horrible,
how Dignity packed her little satchel. She said
of all things, I would most regret telling you how once
I stood before the Temple of Vesta, weeping—
sounds very Eat, Pray, Love, you said—and I do.

Love Poem with Ebb Tide

I mistook strangers' gestures for yours—
strangers walking toward me in the sun. Lilacs

tossed by the wind. The tiny bones

of our wrists sometimes ached when it rained,
and Sundays I bought books and artichokes,

thinking why do I have to be so fragile,

I am too fragile. You held my face
in your fingers. We shielded our eyes

when the harbor was filled with sails. White
sails! And the long breaths of cool wind

from Quebec. I had a feeling someone
was looking for me, but searching the wrong

century. When I went to sea—but I didn't,

I never went. I just stood on the pier.
You walked by, carrying a lantern.

Love Poem with Darkened Lamps

Came a day I stopped caring
if it rained in. You were as absent

from the floorboard gone soft with rot
as you were from the salt-stained

newel posts of the porch. Thunder
hung around the edges of my

county. Came a day the uniform
of gray withstood no more washing.

The lamps burned out and I let
them. I'd never locate you

in the colony of yellowjackets
vibrating in the shade of the eaves,

in the windowsill's ruin
or what remained of the curtain's

white eyelet. Nor could I
find you in the dry rooms

of almost-sleep, or the knobs
of doors my fist closed around.

III.

The weather is a better companion and by that I don't just mean

she looks good in filmy things, she has a humid mouth.
I can believe it on a Sunday when the laundry's clean,
but once I had it in my head to write a book—*The Erotics of Cloud-Watching.*
That urge was ultimately better served by filling a bowl with small yellow pears
and placing it on the windowsill. That urge was a product of drinking
too much salt water. On a Sunday the weather is a better
companion because I'd rather not know when I've been taken.
Rather not see the way our softer impulses can be turned
against us, failures of generosity. In my twenties I learned
a kind of patience called lying in a field watching the sky. Bonus
points for shadows of birds crossing my body. Bonus points
for sentences about the poetics of praxis, the beautiful sentences
beginning with desire and ending with restlessness. It was good practice
for falling in love with a man-shaped theorem. Now I am learning
a kind of patience called afterwards. Bonus points
for not overusing the passive voice. That urge is better served
by studying the cloud dictionary—*cirrostratus nebulosus,*
nimbostratus opacus—and I'd rather not know when I've been lied to.
The weather is a better companion and by that I mean
on a Sunday when the laundry's done I don't ask myself too many
questions; I trust the wide open window and the weather when she enters.

Yellow House Poem

Leave unexcavated from the narrow strip
of garden the Matchbox cars, the Lego astronauts,
the fingers of dolls. Unlistened-to, the zing
of unplugged telephone static and no red windbreakers
snag in the trees. Unpried, the floorboards
between whose sloping joints are collected nickels,
stuck as though through a jukebox slot to needle
the house's hits. Or release cool sugar.
There's a memory in the basement: unpretty, sevenish,
she burns her clothes each evening in the furnace
and is unreachable through Ouija. There's another
in the master bedroom: pregnant wisp holding
her belly. Leave undug the backyard, the base
of the utility pole standing like a priest
with a direct connection to the forces
of electricity, tirades, and greenish skies.
Leave unglassed the windows where rain
leaks in and streaks the walls with exhaust.
There is no creak in the stairs, the teeth
of vacant winters have gnawed the burrows
of historic mice and slivers in the kitchen
collect unswept. Meter-readers do not visit
this street; no fat letters are dropped in the mail slot.
No owl nests in the garage's dry rafters—no wisdom,
no midnight *who;* there are no children here to soothe.

Operative

Disguised as a shadow
I burgled the theater,
blackened the stage sets
and liberated the character shoes.

Disguised as a snow squall
I infiltrated the cold
to set its wide white clocks
running backwards.

It was when I went
disguised as Aphrodite
that I slept around,
drunk on apple schnapps—

but only when I looked
like Artemis was I considered
dangerous: pale and chaste
and wielding a bow.

Disguised as a fox
I lived alone, tending
my red pelt and my raging
hunger. In autumn,

disguised as a boy, I went
among hunters, put the shot
buck's tongue back in his mouth,
kissed his eyes closed.

Ghost Story

At two A.M. the lamp came on
by itself, and I sat in my t-shirt
in the circle of yellow light, asking
the spirit what it wanted. Leaves
shifted in the gutter. How long
have I lived in this house? Long enough
to have worn out my boots, long
enough to have used up the vinegar.
I don't remember very much
from our first autumn here—just
the sound the wind made in the wall
before we had it fixed. We all
have to moan sometimes. We all
need some attention. I made the spirit
a promise: I said I would leave
the lamp on. I said I would stay.
At three A.M. the light clicked off again,
just as I'd begun to drowse and dream
about the characters
from a book I thought I'd forgotten.
I walked back to bed in the dark—
the pads of my feet flat against
the wooden floorboards.
Two white hands floated
before me in the blackness, and
they scared me, even though
I knew they were my own hands.

Diorama

In the Hall of North American Mammals, the wolves
lope across a snow-plain lit by the aurora.

It's a study in blue: sodium and glowing against the black
of the hall's warm velvet. If this were a children's tale

you'd find your way inside, and the wolves
would raise you, marvelous changeling, and you'd grow

wise and wild and strong. But the wolves don't want you
and you're no longer a child. Are those pinpricks, on the surface

of the painting, for the small electric dots
of starlight to shine through? Here's another scenario:

it's the flicker from some flip-side tableau the priests
of this place use to keep the magics balanced:

The girl you were, running, casting a thin, knife-like shadow
as the wolves pursue. Or perhaps just you as you are:

a tired woman who gets up in the night to swallow a pill.
You could stand here all day while the scene makes

its slow dissolve from biology to artifice and back. Blue
as a nightlight, blue as the base of flame. You're waiting

for the final reveal, when the glass wears down
through the sheer force of desire and the creatures

begin their slow, twining call. Or you step up,
into that stage-prop forest, under the colored arch

of the long-ago sky, and walk at last into your actual life.

The Snow House

All afternoon I built my shelter of snow,
and with such intimacy it urged me—the cold—
pines full of the smell of winter,

ghosts cast up by the wind where it touched.
High up the rush of the white sky went one way,
went another, and crows called in the circling crests.

Like other lonely beings I had a song—a long
meandering thing with no tune. Building
the shelter I sang it, star-shaped haws rattling

dry under their skin of frost, the holly berries
glowing red in the dusk like tiny lantern-lights.
Flame-song, needle-song. The shelter

opened its one high-domed room and December
was the lover, pale-eyed and whispering,
who bent with me to enter.

Raven

The raven pacing the white field
was there when I walked up, there still
when I walked down. I was thinking

no one wants to be haunted, but we
go on remembering anyway. I was so cold.
Spring has come but winter won't go—

last night it snowed so the raven
was crossing the white field all morning.
Near that place, where the road forks,

there's a house with a crack in every window.
There's a tree standing in its own scattered ruins
and a ledge where cold water slips

over stone and pools in a scooped basin.
The water tastes of iron. The snow
on the hill tastes of granite, the first violets

of blood. The raven watched me
walk up, walk down. At each step
I thought *I am a body, walking.* I thought,

don't you leave me, raven. Heard
the sound of footsteps shifting the old leaves,
the sough of wind in last year's barley.

Tell your phone to stop calling me

from the bottom of the river.

Tell midnight to stop coming
in strange cities where the bells
sound emptier, and heavy.

Tell Mary her hands are too open already—
she may not have noticed there's no one to fill them.

Your phone has debased itself: its pad of numbers
a set of little soft fingertips sealed
in plastic, its contact list kicked
downstream.

I wished something once—I almost
forget. It had to do with you. It had to do
with the vowels of my name, blue
water warm to sink into.
It didn't work out that way.

Tell the moon I admire it
for conserving its energy.

Tell the river if it wants to talk
there are certain courtesies.
It should empty its mouth of stones.

It should fall on its knees.

Listening to the Dead

I've come unstitched, says the rabbit in the orchard, belly
torn open by dogs. *Maggots have come to sew me back*

into earth. All around, the softening apples
drop when the wind blows and at night deer approach
and lower their slender necks to eat.

I've lost my eyes, says the rabbit,
whose long strong legs lie crossed like a woman's. *But I hear
leaves rustle, and the sound of lifting wings.*

Now the first snow has fallen.
The rabbit says *I can't feel the cold, and something
has chewed away the pads of my paws.*

The clear, dark air is filled with radio signals
from Finland and Peru, voices borne

as far as the empty moon. *Oh, I'm gone,* says the rabbit,
*no lungs, no nose to sniff at the soil's rich iron,
no coat in the rising sun's gold, nor terror, nor tongue.*

Satellite

When I say stone I don't mean
this cleaved hillside, its rocks
broken by blunt machinery, loud
in its tangle. I mean the blue agate
you want to dip your tongue to,
put your mouth around to taste its ocean
and antiquity. You said I go out
like a radio between stations,

sometimes. Static and slack sagging
among signals, a frequency of loss—
a tender place sheared back, raw.
But when I say desire I still mean the river
welling with rain, a tidal estuary—
not the keening of satellites
falling, abandoned to white noise.

The River Child

Once you had a daughter
and you raised her in a house
overlooking the river. She kept
blue butterflies in ivory cages

and bees in hives in the attic.
Each morning crows
waded on the riverbank, cracking
snails. The house shifted, brick

by brick, toward the water.
Is this what it means, to have
a daughter: knowing that below
her bed are two stories

of dust-shot air, then the graves
of otters? You also knew
that in the morning you would
make her toast with honey.

She would wear her striped sweater
to school, a pencil case in her bag.
The pencil case was filled
with the bodies of bees.

Then one night the moon clicked
over the house and the structure
settled its ashy weight. She turned
in her sleep and all the elements

of your life slid like tumblers in a lock,
and you woke up daughterless.
You brushed your hair
in the particulate light, trying

to remember what it was
you'd intended to do, while the roots
of the house rested at last
in the deep warm clay and the bones.

Household Gods

To the God of Insomnia I offered
my milk teeth, to the God of Hunger
my youth. I sacrificed a hair

to the Goddess of Loneliness: burnt
over the candle's flame so it slipped
back in ash and stank, and I was lonely

still, for seven years, until I learned
to let the spiders weave in the stairwell.
God of the Memory of Missing

Bracelets, Goddess of Windows,
I've yet to discover your appeasement.
Goddess of Thirst, I offer my blood

when I'm cut; Goddess of Boredom,
for you I broke the glass. I lost
my motherhood and sacrificed sleep

to the Goddess of Never. Lost the pleasure
of my lungs. To the God of Small Animals,
then, I sacrificed singing, and that brought

the bees. Goddess of Time: I've offered
my palms, my fevers for this blue room,
the jar of golden honey on the shelf.

Afterlife

I could say I've had enough of being hollowed
like this, delivered from the dead only
to find myself an insufficient container
for the love that claimed my resurrection,
like the woman sentenced forever to fill a sieve
with water in the afterlife. I would rather
die, I think, than squander my heart again;
I tell myself I can be content with the pleasures
permitted ghosts: weather, elastic, the alphabet.
I hang a clock the size of a manhole cover
above my bed and chide myself: *waste not, waste not.*
But in the dream you are tender, telling me you'll take it,
the bundle I've been carrying, that the pigeon
nuzzling at my throat is a good, good bird. I could say
I've had enough of being hollowed and it's true—
I'm not a girl anymore, I have better things to do.
I think I can accept this afterlife, but my body wakes up
leaking saltwater, and won't let my ghost-self be.

Departure

Put my ashes in a cookie tin from Canada.
My epitaph: her life was a series of stubbed toes
and tiger cats, the wind fooling around

under her skirt. Moments I was proud
to be human, like seeing a hopscotch course
a full block long. Before I go I will have to gather

my patience: I left it in the fallout
shelter of my grade school during a drill,
adding up the civil defense rations. I could never

make the totals come out right—there was not enough
Kotex for us all to reach adolescence
in the event of nuclear winter. The part of my brain

still occupied with a stranger's unkindness
at the Museum of Wicker will wink out.
Crying between streetlamps. My own name.

Many mornings I've waited a long time
for coffee, queued up with a dozen fidgeting
commuters, all their nervous little phones, thinking

I need this, I need this. I think of the Rapture
when I pull up my socks. I surprise myself,
sometimes, by stepping out of line and slipping away.

Lullaby

Sleep my losses, my darlings, the wind
snags sticky in the trees. Shiver the old bed

under, the armoire to dust and the bats
in their habits. Sleep the body's broken

boatyards, its cravings, its costume.
Dawn is a pale dog pacing.

Sleep my clappers, my spaniels, my chalice,
my mouth. My battered losses harrowed

and fevered. Sleep the soft shallow hallow,
the blister, the interstate, thunder

and satellite, sparrow, my losses, the brain
socket, syringe and sex and the umber.

The moon is a shardsome sailor, the sea
is a blithesome rider. Sleep losses,

sleep grief and plunder, the blooms
and the babes and the ponies and pipes.

Certificates, sugar, and all my losses. Sleep
spider and sieve and passion and bristle,

harvest and fallow and femur and fire,
sleep empty. My losses. Loosen and slumber.

Karin: "I want everybody to come."